DON'T COUNT ME OUT!
UNDERSTANDING MONEY

By: Emily J. Burton
A Product of Bold Butterfly, LLC

BOLD
BUTTERFLY, LLC

COPYRIGHT © 2020 EMILY J. BURTON
All rights reserved.

DON'T COUNT ME OUT
Understanding Money

ISBN: 978-1-7358879-0-6

Disclaimer: This book is not inclusive of all U.S. currency. It is intended to identify the most commonly used bills and coins.

DEDICATIONS

---

*For my babies Christian & Evan,
who will one day, grow into awesome men!
My love for you is priceless.*

*Remember to always reach for the moon;
if you fall, you will still land among the stars!*

---

*With love to my husband, Christopher,
for allowing us to spend all of his money!
We love you to infinity and beyond.
Forever and ever...*

---

*With much love and appreciation to my mother, Betty,
our family's source of spontaneous song creation.*

Christian and his little brother Evan
were playing at home on a rainy day.
Christian asked his mom, "Wouldn't it be cool
if we could get free toys and *never* had to pay?"

His mom said, "Yes that would be awesome!
Every parent would love to save money!"
That's when Evan asked, "What's money?!"
His mom laughed, "Let me explain it to you honey!"

Money is what we use
in exchange for something else.
Once we make a trade with money,
we can keep it for ourselves.

Whenever we need food and clothes,
we use money for that!
Whenever we buy gifts and toys,
we use money for that!

Everything has a price.
It could be a little or a lot.
What you can afford to buy
depends on how much money you've got.

Christian jumped up and shouted,
"Mommy let's teach him our song!
If he remembers our money song,
then he can't go wrong!"

♪♫   Money! Money!   ♪♫

Now scream and shout!

Money! Money!

Let's count it out!

Dollar bills are the paper – the paper form of money.

ONES,

FIVES,

TENS,

TWENTIES,

FIFTIES,

and
HUNDREDS!

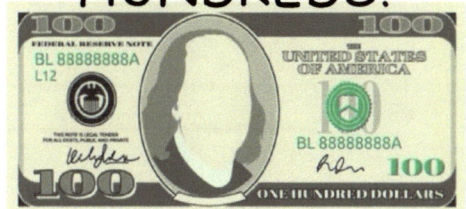

Then you have the coins – the noisy form of money.

 PENNIES,

 NICKELS,

 DIMES,

and

 QUARTERS!

Pennies are worth 1 cent.

Nickels are worth 5!

Dimes are worth 10 cents.

Quarters - 25!

Money! Money!

Now scream and shout!

Money! Money!

Let's count it out!

Coins equal to a dollar,
if you have enough.
You just get them all together,
then you add 'em up!

If you have 100 pennies,
then you have a dollar!

If you have 20 nickels,
then you have a dollar!

If you have 10 dimes,
then you have a dollar!

If you have 4 quarters,
then you have a dollar!

Bills can equal to another.
It depends on the amount.
First you find your largest bill,
then the smaller bills you count!

♪♩ ♪♩ ♪♩

If you have 100 Ones,
then you have 100 dollars!

If you have 20 Fives,
then you have 100 dollars!

If you have 10 Tens,
then you have 100 dollars!

If you have 5 Twenties,
then you have 100 dollars!

Money! Money!
Now I can count!
Money! Money!
Don't Count Me Out!

Christian and Evan danced and sang,
while they continued to play.
Their mom smiled saying, "I can always count on
you guys to brighten up a dark and rainy day!"

COMING SOON

Understanding Money is the first book in the *Don't Count Me Out* series. The following book in the series – *Earning and Saving Money* – will continue the conversation, with the intention of getting children excited about financial literacy. This series will provide a platform for the necessary discussions many families never have with their children and prepare children for a successful financial future.

For more information, email boldbutterflyllc@gmail.com.

ABOUT THE AUTHOR

Emily J. Burton is a proud native of Pine Bluff, Arkansas, where she obtained both her grade school and college education. Emily received her bachelor's degree in Accounting from the University of Arkansas at Pine Bluff, and later obtained her master's degree in Accounting with concentration in Audit from Kaplan University.

After getting married and having two boys of her own, Emily's writing topics began to shift. Her goal is to inspire not only her children, but all children to follow their dreams – no matter how big or small!

Emily was inspired at an early age to write, after reading poetry written by her mother. She took her love of writing, music, and family engagement, and started a business focused on her passion for writing.

Emily is the proud owner of Bold Butterfly, LLC. The mission of Bold Butterfly – through creative writing and self-expression – is to create an environment filled with empowerment, to encourage change that inspires, and to provide hope for a beautiful future. Connect with Bold Butterfly at www.boldbutterflyllc.com, and like us on Facebook and Instagram.

www.ingramcontent.com/pod-product-compliance
Lightning Source LLC
Chambersburg PA
CBHW041800040426
42447CB00001B/37